JUST THIS

JUST THIS

BRIAN TURNER

VICTORIA UNIVERSITY PRESS

TE WHARE WĀNANGA O TE ŪPOKO O TE IKA A MĀUI

VICTORIA UNIVERSITY PRESS
Victoria University of Wellington
PO Box 600 Wellington
http://www.victoria.ac.nz/vup

National Library of New Zealand Cataloguing-in-Publication Data

Turner, Brian, 1944–
Just this / Brian Turner.
ISBN 978-0-86473-591-1
I. Title.
NZ821.2—dc 22

Printed by Printlink, Wellington

For my son, André

Acknowledgements

Grateful thanks to the New Zealand *Listener, Otago Daily Times, Quadrant* and *Sport,* in which some of these poems previously appeared; and to Gilbert van Reenen for the cover photographs.

Contents

I

II

III

IV

V

We can be said only to fulfil our destiny in the place that gave us birth.

William Hazlitt in 'On Going on a Journey', 1822

A person's life purpose is nothing more than to rediscover, through detours of art, or love, or passionate work, those one or two images in the presence of which his . . . heart first opened.

Albert Camus

I

Epistemologies of Place

There's a side to beauty
that is sadness enduring.

There's a belief in beauty
that's peculiarly universal

while unique in itself
to this punter, or that.

It's more the idea
than the actuality

of this place, not who
had the idea for it

that becomes a reality
previously unimaginable.

First there's the perception,
then the journey towards

understanding that comes,
you're told, with empathy;

and, finally, it's the where
you know that refines

the who you are. It's then,
you could say, landscape's

indifference in itself
mirrors our impermanence,

has no awareness of the dramas
which, paradoxically, heighten

and enhance the sense of the
numinous in nuance and hue.

In other words, *you* choose
what it is that makes for piety

and pleasure, and obligation,
and how you measure such,

and what is meant by home,
and why, or whether

you believe, before
your time's up, that

this big, unloved, untidy
unwalled room is it.

Improving for the Worse

I come from New Zealand.
Most people don't know where it is,
or what it stands for. Good.

Nor do most New Zealanders,
if they ever did. Sad.

All of us are islands, entirely lost,
pretending we are not.

What It's Like

When someone asks you to explain
what it's like where you come from
you say you're still finding out,
and it's not because you enjoy being
vague, or smart-arse, a sophist
if you like, it's just because it's true.

This morning frost then fog-like smoke
from a damp wood fire, then the sun
breaking through in lamé-like patches
until there's not even bandannas
left on the hills, and order's restored:
blue sky above incandescent snow.

Goodbye Uncle

When he said he felt as if
he was *going south* in a big way,
it wasn't the same as saying
he was *going down south*
where he was born
and should have stayed.

A friend took one look at him
and told me he was buggered,
on his way any day.

Going south: that's what
my father meant when he said
*I thought they were going
to beam me up yesterday.*

Going south: it's where,
all our lives, we've heard
it is 'behind the times', that
there was 'nothing there,
nothing to do'.

Nothing there? Nobody home, eh?
Just us, who they felt sorry for.

In a Sponsor's Tent

Once I set my mind to it
it wasn't that difficult to be affable
instead of distant, sombre, severe.
As James Salter wrote,
of his last moments at West Point,
'I found myself shaking hands
with men I had sworn not to.'
And I thought, Why not?
None are flawless, all
are fated to fall. There is
an immense brotherhood
that one wishes to belong to,
in spite of oneself, deep down.

Soon I shall again wing south
to that inalienable land
wherein one's sense of solitude
is thrilling and riddling
for what it says about
the us in me, the more we think
of unexplainable things.

Wind

You hear the wind
before you feel it,
see it harassing
defenceless leaves
and listen to limbs creak.

The rowan's suddenly a mass
of nervy red light, the agapanthus
plots of antic asterisks,
the tulips swaying back and forth
like worshippers about to speak

in tongues. The wind's a ferret
angry in the grass,
a cuff on the ear,
an irritant tousling one's hair.

Wind and Stars

Stars do it for us, and yet
when you read where another reckons
'we notice . . . the wind among the stars'
you think that sounds a bit far-fetched.
We notice the stars among the stars
and their seeming absence
throughout the day. Apart from that,
what else? The way the wind spurs
the clouds, and the way the mountains
won't get out of the way.

August, Ida Valley

If you think about it
you could say
life is truth disturbed
by fictions we prefer,

and time wasting for some
is, as Mary Wesley
observed, 'going to bed
with old Etonians',

or not playing sport
for money in the mad
bad 21st of many
similar centuries.

Yet somehow, after
the 10th snowfall
since late April, it seems
winter just won't go away,

sheep still have nothing
to eat but hay, and the
few hawks left are unwilling
to turn a blind eye.

Snow in September

Someone I've yet to meet
is playing a violin in the snow
in a field nearby
and it sounds like Beethoven
to me, and under the willows
by the stream
a young boy is weeping.
When the music stops
the boy will disappear
as he does every time,
every time.

When

When you're in the sky
the land's all over the place
as if it's been dropped
from a scary height
and is still trying to
work out how to get
comfortable.
          When on land
the sky's always there,
dressing and undressing,
never short of clothes
or room to parade them in,
and always insatiable for air.

November Snow
(after Bill McKibben's *Wandering Home*)

When snow is falling straight down
on coarse grass that's already brown,
the fire is fluttering,
and some mezzo is singing

a lament on the radio,
it's easy to go with the flow
of gilded memories . . . of times
that ring like rhymes.

There's the smell of wood smoke,
too, a frog's quavery croak,
and a scent that can only be thyme
whose aroma is near sublime . . .

and I think, when we say complete
we don't mean tidy, neat;
we mean order, what's appropriate,
the sane, mature passage of fate.

That is what we hunger for
from youth to drear death's door,
to gather a sense of relief
equally as strong as grief.

It's learning how to say goodbye,
to bury the lies where you lie,
to have made a certain private space
that you can claim to be your place.

Foretold
(for Vincent and Helen)

There's a warm breeze blowing down
off the mountains
now that most of the snow has gone.

There's a song somewhere
in the heart of every man and woman
with the heart to sing.

There's elation born of relief
and the return of hope and grace
in the flight of a hawk over Rough Ridge.

There's beauty in the unruffled
olive green and grey feathers of silver-eyes
feeding on sugar on my schist stone wall.

There's rivers and streams that are
quieter again, and sheep and cattle
whose stoicism never falters.

There's the feeling exile's over,
and that, for all its limitations,
what's foretold has barely begun.

Full Moon in November

Orange and hearty in the fullness
of another month gone round.

There's tubular cloud couching the moon
smirking above the Hawkduns,

Venus bright in the tops of the birch
next-door, the leaves of an oak shuffling,

quelling anxiety; and across the road
one bare streetlight set to shine

until daylight returns. I go to bed
with Fauré's *Requiem* playing

in another room, moonlight milder
than the frenzied importuning of stars.

December Drought

The grasses are wispy, the land's blond,
rivers mere streams, creeks dry.

Sheep scavenge, eat straw and stones
and the edges show through their skin.

Every bird's a rival by every dwindling pond.
Winds chap and burn. Far off, clouds

huddle in the ranges and deny us rain.
At night the sky's black and sprinkled

with all the stars this side of infinity
and, miles away, in small-time towns

and on parched farms, those you've never met
gather to chant Abide, abide, abide . . .

East

The brightest star I can see tonight is dead
    so astronomers and physicists say,

when explaining their understanding
    of matters to do with illumination and . . .

I wouldn't know, except to hope
    beauty's for everyone, one way

or another; in the shapes of ducks
    flying across the face of the moon,

or in the hues of bales of hay
    lying in paddocks docile in sunlight,

in cirrus stretched over the mountains, in
    insects scritching in bone-dry grass.

Just This

'Find your place on the planet, dig in,
and take responsibility from there.'
    Gary Snyder

Affecting without affectation, like the sere hills
then the early evening sky where Sirius dominates
for a time, then is joined by lesser lights,

stars indistinct as those seen through the canopies
of trees shaking in the wind. There's this wish
to feel part of something wholly explicable

and irreplaceable, something enduring
and wholesome that suppresses the urge to fight . . .
or is there? Ah, the cosmic questions

that keep on coming like shooting stars
and will, until, and then what? All I can say
is that for me nothing hurts more

than leaving and nothing less than coming home,
when a nor'wester's gusting in the pines
like operatic laughter, and the roadside grasses

are laced with the blue and orange and pink
of bugloss, poppies and yarrow, all of them
swishing, dancing, bending, as they do, as we do.

Honestly

There's a bit battered
wool-buyer's truck in Omakau
that has painted on a plate
hanging on the tailgate
the words 'Nearly Honest Brent'.

That could stand as
a worldwide epitaph
and for reasons
inexplicable
I'm reminded

of my father's
last words to me
which were not
'I did my best', but
'the soup looks good'.

Put Down

When you shot the horse
you said you hoped
it would go straight down
and not stand there
as if deciding whether
to begin a dressage routine.

And someone who claimed
to know horses
said the animal knew
what was coming,
the slash between its eyes
like forked lightning.

Moving Stock

A curdle of sheep wobbles by
leaving freckles
and liver spots
all over the road.

On the Road to Wedderburn

Snow and ice and a sniping wind
    so the dead hare's ropy-red entrails
are sustenance for a hawk
    defiant in desperation.

In the wind it's minus 6, minus 9
    an hour ago. The bird's close
to going the way of the hare
    who knew the now but not

the now we know. In the way
    one does for reasons of conscience
and compassion, I swerve so as
    not to mow the bird down,

wave and wish him all the blood
    and guts he can stand.

In the Hill's Creek Cemetery

Everything says tenuous here
    where neat edging and vases of fresh flowers
are one way of trying to tidy untidy lives,

and even the empty jars
    that shine in the morning sun reflect remembrance
in all its kaleidoscopic fragmentations:

love, affection, grief . . . guilt
    about inattention when it was needed most,
apologies not made, churlishness enjoyed,

schadenfreude relished, and so on.
    What matters most can't be attended to now
in a place where guilt and sincerity

are determined to merge as self-indulgence.
    But never mind, if we're lucky the road to hell
may not be paved with good intentions

here or anywhere else, and,
    in a soak close by, a heron practises dressage,
paradise ducks pretend imperious, and above us all

a hawk masters disdain. Dry grass wafts.
    Serenity's hanging on somehow despite pervasive
evidence of our mortality and, overhead, the wisps of cirrus

that tell us a big nor'wester's not far way.

Between Shingle Creek and Fruitlands

Cast your mind back to the first time you came this way,
    the road windy, corrugated, dusty,
the surface mostly the colour of yellow clay, cuttings
    stained with the leer of water seeping.

On the left the ever-ascending slopes,
    the Old Man Range, white flecks
in blue gullies near the summit,
    and your young old man wondering when

we'd *ever* get to Alexandra, your mum complaining
    about 'the blessed dust', both of them
cursing the 'washboard surface' and you thinking
    about the number of times she told your father

that 'it didn't matter' when it clearly did. And that
    was the way it always was with them,
it is with you, it is, period. Until, you might say,
    something happens that's never happened before.

Like love came back and sent hate packing
    never to return, and peace of mind arrived
like a dove from afar, decided to stay, and you
    no longer dreamed of what might have been.

Shapes of the Wind

Wherever there's said to be nothing
you'll find something
you never knew before.

Cadence in a desire to do the right thing
for the right reasons;
principle that isn't sourced

in righteousness; hope and optimism
that isn't misplaced,
based on ignorance or naivety;

somethings you can have faith in,
swear by. And if, after a while,
nothing seems to have arrived

and quirked the mind, lie back
in the springy grasses
and watch clouds like surplices;

there you'll see the shapes of the wind.

Theatre Country

Call it landscape, call it scenery,
    or call it theatre country.
Talk of how awesome, how majestic,
    or how picturesque
it is; of the mauri, the numinous,
    the spiritual, whatever fits
whatever you think you have in mind . . .
    the perception's cultural, the aura
personal. That's it, isn't it? In that sense
    nothing's changed, and nothing will,
evidently.
        To some it looks like the land's
not 'performing' in the strut-like
    sense of the term, and that
it's our performance that counts,
    when and how we come to see it.
Look, the bones in the graveyards
    hereabouts, how do we discern
what sort of impact each performer had
    in a place where the nor'westers
blow so hard they topple headstones
    and send iron sheets whirling
like dervishes though not in ecstasy.
    Look, on hillsides lie the skeletons
of other creatures whose passings are
    randomised, unrecorded. So maybe
we can't call it theatre country after all
    unless theatrics are arcane productions
rehearsed elsewhere, showcased here.

Humpty Dumpty

A celestial Humpty Dumpty, a full moon
squatted on top of Mt Ida

and when leaving the pub
my mate said, *Wow, look at that*

great orange lozenge. Another stammered,
Holy hell, a rococo show

if ever there was one. Meanwhile
my neighbour Clarkey

was hard at it chainsawing rounds
that lay about gleaming like moons.

Deserts, for instance

The loveliest places of all
are those that look as if
there's nothing there
to those still learning to look

Mercurial Michael in the Maniototo

A poet I know better than most drove a borrowed Mercedes
all the way from Earnscleugh to Oturehua, up the Ida,

the Hawkduns surreal at the head of the valley, the blue sky
full of cast-off scarves white as cavaliers'. It wasn't his own,

of course, for what would a poet be doing with a Merc, except
wondering, yet again, about the need for such sophistication,

querying the enduring worth of the so-called best money can buy?
Give me a manual floor shift any day, he said, *no fancy locks,*

and windows you can wind down by hand. And as he drove away,
and tooted and waved, insouciant and feeling silly,

the way you do because you get that round here, do you what,
I thought, *You're dead right, mate, that's my fuckin' boy.*

Red Tractor

A dinky   red tractor
tows a plough   up and down
an umpteen-hectare   paddock. The exhaust's

a cheroot puffing sporadically. Checkered gulls
yo-yo behind, land and take off repeatedly,
crankiness and competition synonymous
when the mechanical means meals,
birds bugging bugs
where the road towards the uplands
turns away from downland, curves like the one cloud

tilted above   the ranges
that is, for the   moment, edged
with crimson   and yellow.

Blue Herons in the Evening

Blue-grey wings the colour of scree
on late summer afternoons;

wing-beats slow as flags flapping
in a drifter, two herons in flight

in the twilight in front of the glowing
white and gold snow on the Hawkduns . . .

can one safely assume they are never going
to want to blame or take issue with

the behaviour of the sun, the moon,
and the stars? Most probably

is the answer I give in the absence
of anyone else to ask. But don't

misinterpret me, aloneness isn't
loneliness. There's smoke rising

from the chimney of my small house
as I walk slowly home, the skyline

of Blackstone Hill jagged, sharp-etched,
assured, the air clean, chill, fresh

and me, for once, not limping or labouring
under the weight of a need for exoneration.

Some Basic Facts

One moment the sky is clear as benediction,
the next there's snowflakes in the air,

and whatever you'd banked on, innocently,
then ignorantly – enduring love, or fewer

fuck-ups, say – is overwhelmed by the brevity
that scoffs at eternity, Methusalah in drag.

Sky

If the sky knew half
of what we're doing
down here

it would be stricken,
inconsolable,
and we would have

nothing but rain

Last Outing

She waited for him to come home,
knowing where he was
yet wondering just the same.

He was on the hill, among
the grey, lichen-braised rocks,
the creamy, straw-coloured grasses,

in a world where clouds
defer to blue sky, and hawks
are as much languor as threat

in flight. A world where sheep
look at you as if querying
your right to be there, and quail

behaviour is snickery, irascible.
As the sun went down she knew
the far hills reminded him

of all they hadn't done as much
as what they had, in their place,
together, the evening light

that haunts the way home does.

Fisherman

When the fisherman found
he could no longer row his dinghy
the tide went out in his heart,

and when I asked him what he felt
about that, he said he didn't know
where to start. You'll have to . . .

he said, but didn't complete
the sentence about a sentence
because he'd already said it all.

II

In a South Dunedin Garden

My dad's dad, Louis, looked after his tools,
    his implements. He sharpened chisels
        and saws, cleaned the head of his hammer

till it gleamed like a glans. He tapped shovels
    and spades on the toe of a dusty boot,
        and hosed the last of the dirt off until the metal

shone as the sun smarted there, a fiery
    approbation and an answering leer.
        And then he went and washed his hands

in a big-bellied tub in the garden shed.
    We washed in the same water, my thin
        white and his rough-skinned fingers

writhing and squirming like fledglings
    in a nest. Waste not, want not, he said
        again and again every week of my childhood.

He taught me the simpler things that
    can be overlooked, like leaving carrots
        in the ground until their tassely tops

announce their readiness, and allowing
    potatoes weeks if need be to show off
        their piquant flowers. And that the washing

up afterwards, of face and hands, of food
    for the table, was necessary conviviality
        as much for others' sakes as for oneself.

It's all about respect, he said, and gratitude.
    That sort of statement of virtue I could live with
        for it seemed to make sense, even then.

Journey

I've got my old jalopy, sure have,
it's the heart in my mouth

when I see dust on the horizon,
a blue haze over the mountains

and the evening sky
a multi-coloured dream coat.

What's wrong with that?
How often do you have to give

what you can? How often
is enough? Riding high

on a four-wheeler and rocking,
what a journey it was

sitting up there beside your grandfather
when your father was young.

First Day of School

The small boy
holds his father's hand
tightly, David

at the school gates
with a benign
Goliath.

Neither is keen
to let go
before the bell tolls.

Joy

He knew what joy is,
    the urge
to break into a run
      to greet a son
returning home.

Like Father, Like Son

He told me what his father looked like
but not what he believed or why.

He hadn't seen the him in him.
Some things are too hard.

Father and Son

I never wanted to be like him,
    and he would not
have so much as thought
    of being seen
as an older version of me.

That's how I saw it anyway.
    If we never grew closer,
did we grow further apart?
    Only I could answer that,
and I can't, *I can't.*

Fear

I can tell you what fear is
and when it started.
It's a policeman's little black book
and what goes down in it.

Your father told you about it
and the consequences
of misdemeanour, that crimp,
which became the book

that grows under your skin,
watermarks of conscience throughout,
contrition sharp as barley grass
in your socks, and like confessions

hard to extract. 'Experience
is the best teacher,' Dad said,
'and we're part of yours,'
Mum added, her eyes the colour of peat,

except when joy dismissed
anguish whereupon they turned
biscuit-brown, then lightened,
shone like acorns. You don't find

peace there – at least I didn't,
and haven't – when you're downcast
like a colt without shoes
standing in the fitful shade.

Open Road

At the end of the open road
there's an open road.

There's a girl playing in a ditch
where tadpoles flicker like pounamu.

Her dress is sky blue
and there's a red ribbon

in her golden hair:
her mummy calls her dear.

There's a grubby boy
peeking through the hedge,

downwind as his father
taught him when hunting deer

and pigs. He lives on a farm.
His father shot himself last year.

The girl is singing sweetly,
'Jesus loves me yes I know

for the Bible tells me so.'
She has faith and no knowledge

of fear or favour. The boy
has undone his fly.

The myth is that
at the end of the open road

they have all the time in the world
and the world cares.

North Dunedin

You turn into the short, blind street,
its four houses and the back end of a factory
that made jellies, essences and instant coffee,
and stop in front of the two-storey wooden place
that was *home* for a time in the 1950s.
It still leans a bit to the north
as if cocking its ears, listening for reports
from parts of the country *up there*
where there's said to be greater material prosperity
and worse poverty, conflict disguised as cultural diversity.
New Zealand's 'social laboratory'
wasn't meant to turn out like this. Bugger.

So what's truly changed here except the rate
of acceleration? Students have tacked a sign,
'Hotel California', below an upstairs window
in a room that served as your mother's kitchen.
Inside someone's playing a CD of something
heavy the whole street is required to hear –
and you recall it was here that your father
first introduced you to Mahler, hooked you
and alienated his mother for the umpteenth time.
So it goes, but why God only knows.

You're on a tour, visiting houses once called home
in other parts of this resilient southern town, in
St Kilda, Corstorphine, Musselburgh, Mornington . . .
where memories resuscitate more than connive
when you see that the houses are no less serviceable
than before. And then you leave, go inland
where absence in abundance still reigns
and people yearn to fill it, drive back
to a place you'd love to call *home*.

Farewell
(i.m. Brian Shea)

A man I liked a lot is dying in his bedroom
    a hundred yards away from me,
on a day when the clouds over the mountains
    are indigo in the morning sun
and inwardly fuming. A gale is shaking blossom
    to the ground, the pines are thrashing,
hoo-ing and haa-ing, and my study window
    is rattling. This weather's something to do
with the equinox, perhaps, or perhaps not.
    My provisional tax bill has just arrived,
but my friend knows none of this, or of any
    other certainty any more. His family waits
surrounded by hush and realities that hark
    as I scrawl these words, Granados's
Epílogo in the background. And the wind gusts,
    abates, and gusts, again and again.

A Wry Big Bloke

(i.m. Dexter Valentine)

1

One of your colleagues delivered the first eulogy
'and pretty damned gloomy it was, too,'
said another, cycling, friend who gave the other

on behalf of our club members. And three days later,
while we were riding our bikes towards Portobello,
the sea crisping on the stone wall, the sun blinding

at heaven's gate, he said, 'I was thinking, Dexter
would have said, "I've gone, there's nothing
you can do, so get on with it."' True,

and all very well, but what to do about
phrases that badger us: before one's time;
taken too early; a crying shame; end of the line.

And gone, gone where? At such times free will's
a piffling phrase and no one's in command
while we remain but one blink away from eternity.

2

To set a good example's all very fine
but any example's better than none at all
irrespective of what the righteous say.

Language tells us that no one's straightforward,
nothing's as simple as it seems,
and that language itself keeps us alive.

We are into myth here, myth which jockeys truth
and is always dawning, not conclusive,
never final, not particular at all.

3
Do not query language, query with it.
Waive if you must, but do not waver.
If you must be sly, do not expect

grandiose applause when you argue the point.
Do not think language will hold you
in high regard, or save you; that

the written word is more reliable
or powerful, will guarantee your legacy.
The spoken's what terrifies.

4
Squint through language, angle, feint.
Joust, enjoin, fare away; count
your lucky stars if you pick up the notes

rather than the reasons. Meditation's
the medium, language the message,
an old fandangle fandangling.

5
Cloud-roamer, dreamer, when you feel
some part of you is flying
you know you're one with the best you'll be.

Or so you would have it, only a stone's throw
away from the throne-room
where the spirit and the soul

are hands lightly clasped
in tolerance instead of admonition,
irreligious as modesty.

6

We're on our way now, the fretful
passing of the years cordoned off,
and the slack between the tides

is like that sere moment
when a horse is flying, hooves
in the air, and the dust

that spurts, then spreads
as if the earth's breath is
thickened sunlight, is a kind

of petit mort, and when
you shut your eyes you can
see what you hear

and the sky's windblown
like the sea foaming
on the isles of Paradise.

Precursors to Sleep

Listen to others, my mother said,
        meaning who or what? Perhaps that
the noise lambs make in the evenings
    sounds like crying, whereas
in the chorusing of birds we hear
       echoing the origin of all things.

Listen to others . . . of course, but who?
      Any one of a dozen so-called leaders
driven by expediency, pragmatism, vanity?
      Who knows? Or someone who, like Balzac,
believed the young could choose
      only one of three paths: obedience,

struggle or revolt? There are other options
      one supposes. And so my choice tonight
is to sit outside watching the sun
    bright on the leaves of the oak, the rowan,
the birch and the willow, a quorum
      quivering in the ailing breeze;

is to choose to stay here and look and listen
      until the sun goes down, goodbye, and
the bands of cirrus over the mountains are livid
    and striped like bacon. And when stars appear
scattered like dice and sleep's inevitable instead
      of opportune, I choose to acquiesce, goodnight.

Something That's Yet to Come Your Way

Of course, of course you would feel
a need to say it, listening
to Sibelius, his images, sounds
conjuring pictures of geese
passing over, laboured-seeming
yet lovely, rhythmic. It makes you
want to believe the earth's
a constant and will be for
evermore. Oh, dreamer, oh
optimist against all the odds.

But you can't forget the earth's
apparent constancy, eerie
yet consoling in summer
when nights are balmy
and moths clutter on the windows;
eerie and fierce when frost
is rimy on winter nights,
freezing fret because you have
to get by somehow or other.

On the clearest nights
the sky is full of dice
and significant is a word
denoting something darkly trite
when what's to be
and what will be
seem one and the same.

It's then the true self's seen
as a work in progress, querulous
and equivocal, no question,
hesitant more than decisive.
And there's always
that longing for something
that's yet to come your way.

Sailing to the Is-Land

Once, in a temperate time,
  we set out
sailing for the is-land

but I can't remember why.
  I only know
the ground swell was heavy

and the sea was a Prussian blue
  with sea birds
flecking and calling. And veering

south a lip of white
  curling to the beach
and the sky a memory.

We went together, a breeze
  scurrying, you saying
I wonder if this is wise.

We hardened sheets, came
  on the wind.
A slight heel on starboard tack

and we cleared the point
  cleaving, water
washing the hull to the toe-rail,

the log ticking. And before
  long we were well
offshore, just the two of us,

the one I was, and the one
  I'm not, somewhere
between the horizon ahead

and the horizon astern,
    the is–land
more where than here.

Libraries

To arrange a library is to practise,
in a quiet and modest way,
the art of criticism.
—Borges

From every shelf there's a ticking,
    a pulse, respect for the integrity
in exploration through language,
    measured by the music, the cadence
in the arrangement and meaning
    of words, sly or brash, subtle or blunt,
where plainness, striving to simplify
    the complex, can be loveliest
and golden like grace. And when
    unexpected images startle and please
there's instruction made painless
    by the feel, the look, the elegant
functionality of the rectangles
    that package attempts to formulate
profound expressions. Times when
    the light on the spines reminds you
of evenings when the sky in flames
    is redolent, a reliquary of a universe
that is golden, and the whole conveys
    what's immortal in the mind.

III

Chances of Revelation
(at Big Bay, August 2001)

1
What lies in front of us
that isn't a lie? What spreads above
that isn't empty of all
but our illusions?

Why shouldn't the sight
of familiar places
fill us with joy
and, sometimes, invoke

melancholy and nostalgia
as well as glad memories?
Why is sadness
the flipside of happiness,

and could we live
with one only? Isn't
there more than either/or,
more than winners

or losers? Don't insist
that choice is a right
or a given: we're not
required to be saintly,

just appreciative,
and to look for the art in,
or of . . . or else forego life's
chances of revelation.

2
You may be a liar
at times, in some ways,
but you're not deluded
to the point where
you'd claim your life
was in order
like a few of your friends
were tempted to,

implying you ought
to note they hadn't
made as many stuff-ups
as you. Hardly
illuminating though true,
so how is it
you can't accept
they're really worthier than you?

3
It's nice to be musical,
good too. To make,
one hopes, pleasing
sounds, rather than

discordant noises:
the awful stuff
you'd sooner not hear.
The trouble is,

others do, their ears
different from yours.

4
The thing about old lovers
is you can't say
they're pretty any more.
It's a bugger.

And they can't say
you're as good-looking
either . . . or did they, ever?
That's a bugger, too.

5
Don't give me *only* anything.
Some of this and some
of that'll do, and I'll
come up with . . .

you never know what,
but it'll be
different, or so
one supposes.

6
Are you bent?
A bit.
Are you contrite?
Now and then.

Have you ever
been a hit?
Dunno, but you
very much doubt it.

So when you
find out what's what
you'll know . . .
how much?

7
Surely it's not a lie
to say you'd make do
with the blessed sound
of running water,

a breeze in the tall trees,
the last of the sunlight
bronze on the ruckled forest,
a patina on the slopes

of Red Mountain in the east
that's worthy of notice
in the sense
it's of no serious consequence.

8
It's said a poet's a poet
when scarcely himself,
though it's beyond
the himself that's the collection

of recollection that
trips him up, the things
(or thinks) he thinks
he thinks, the buzz

that stops him saying
what he was going to
because he's not sure
what good it will do.

9
You were advised
many times to *commit,*
not to half-arse it,
which is good in theory

as long as the theory's
sound, but not when
the cry Holus Bolus
turns out to be

almost an
ethical injunction.

10
You haven't tricked anyone,
aren't tricked out
and hot to trot. Trit-trot,
trit-trot, it makes

a non-threatening sound.
But trot-trit, ah, you hear that
once only, and never want
to hear it again.

11
In some ways
adding's better
than subtraction,
for you're going

to be deleted
before long . . .
though you could argue
pruning beats planting

when the choice
is yours. You know
what *the* problem is?
It's the urge

to take control,
and by refusing
to take part
you lose.

12
When you're outside
in the sun, seated
in an old brown armchair
in your little porch,

a deer fencepost
holding the roof up,
drinking black coffee
and eating the chocolate

biscuits that are bad
for you, music's playing
all over the place —
magpies, merinos, huntaways,

and a miscellaneous
collection of small
avians whose noise
is disproportionate

to their size. It's enough
to say Hi to happiness,
to vow to try to persist
in staying alive.

13
Little but questions, questions, questions.
For instance, why so many conventions?
Why acts requiring apologies?
Why maladies instead of melodies?
Why the weak battered by the strong?
Why do we keep getting it wrong?

14
Don't even think about trying
to define *identity* as such —
say you've enough trouble
with your own. Say there's
difference and there's similarity
and not much in between. *No.*

You swing, turn like a weather vane,
and every time someone says
aim for consistency, you shrink
from view. You know the ideal –
supposing that were it – is
not possible for you, not because

you're a loser, always, but because
faith's an hourglass
and complexity rules. So pray
that others might respect you
for the right reasons, for yourself,
perhaps, when you find it.

15
Horace Walpole was said to have been
a genius for gossip, to have had
'an outsider's soul with an insider's access'.

Great. Gossip's everywhere ubiquitous
but the problem is
the purpose to which it's put.

16
You write, in part,
and mindful always
that all is qualification

until The End, to explain
yourself to yourself
and give others their due.

17
You take it there'll be
something to see tomorrow
that you haven't seen before.

Your neighbour's bare arse
at the window? Nah, not.
Sheep that talk sense,

or a strange bird
in the lilac 'bent by'
flight 'coincident'

singing outside your window;
a young man
with straw in his hair

and a belief in beauty
pursued by a woman
who doesn't think

the problems of the world
are caused by males;
and a morning like?

Like no other when
nothing further's required
to be taken further.

18
The private man
is often oddly different
from the public man
says Chesterton
making it hard
to disagree.

You think it's not
what you say about
yourself that lasts
longest, but what
others say that strikes
others as memorable

be it true or false.
As when Chesterton
said of Alice Meynell
that she was not 'shadowy'
or 'fugitive', 'She was
a message from the sun'.

19
Both the worst
and the best thing
about being a poet
is, as Jung said,

his 'work means more
to him than his fate'.

20
Distance is distance,
it neither sees nor hears
nor looks any way.

It speaks, though, and haunts
like the welling in Borodin's
Steppes of Central Asia

where distance becomes
the space between
a dog chasing a rabbit

and the nearest burrow,
between a falcon diving
and the finch's darting eye.

21
You live in a valley that doesn't seem
much like a valley to those
who don't live here, because
the hills on either side

don't look high or steep,
and they're not, until
you're on them and the effort
needed to climb them hits you
as the views do, far and wide:
and because the valley too
is pretty flat except for the few
unimposing old river terraces
easily overlooked as you fly by.

But that's the Ida, you say,
and you like it because
of what doesn't catch the eye
when you drive through quickly:
pieces of sky captured in ponds,
mailboxes to farms you'll not notice,
everywhere the innocuous
assuming more significance.

22
'We are ourselves
pools in a long brook,'
says Ammons, who is, presumably,
more honest with us,
and himself, on paper
than in person.
He's not alone there.
I fear I may be a bit the same,
and it makes me feel
part of a team
whose members are told about it
by self-appointed selectors.
Like rivers at noon in high summer
we glisten, we mumble, mutter.
And when we take
a shine to the world
it takes a shine to us.

23
Spring Nor'wester

When the nor'wester blows in the night
you lie in bed and say it's
the whole world's bullies and blusterers
hard at it under cover of darkness,
the time of cowards. And when it stops
and you go outside to see
what's caught on fences and snagged
on bushes, what's lying around
on paths and roads, you're at a loss to explain
why your one wish is to meditate
rather than mediate, as time does,
as earth complies. Accept that melancholy's
only one part of your life
and happiness the other.

24
Heavenwards

Don't expect whatever's or whoever's
up there has a sense of obligation
to any of us. After all, who's heard back?

How much room is there? And who
gets priority? Let's just say
today would be a pretty good day

to make for the Pearly Gates, and,
would that, when the time comes,
you've a choice of hour, a choice

of weather, a choice of light,
and your heart's less heavy,
and your eyes are bright

with the fanfare of a full life.

25
Chicken or the Egg

It was his fault,
he changed.
It was her fault,
she changed.
Both have truth
on their side.
It's a win–win
situation
that no one wins.

26
One trudges on. Stops here
and there. Scratches
and scuffs, signs of wear
and tear. One unlatches
gates and crosses fields,
then pauses, till time yields.

IV

Unfashionable Suggestions

There are a few things you could do
    to protect what's left of your sanity.
For instance, put honour and integrity

on a pedestal and chuck doubt,
    equivocation, vanity, filth and degredation
into the offal pit. Go back and watch

the last episode of *The Singing Detective*
    first, and whenever you meet Janus
tell him you haven't time to audition for

reality TV shows, or call Adam Parore Mortgages,
    say you're off to meet St Francis because
you've heard he has better, unfashionable

things to offer. Like the possibility of tranquility,
    confidence stripped of conceit, a calming air
when your heart's sounding like a timpanum.

Lifestylers Anonymous

You remember the people who made their pile
and moved out of town
    to live a more peaceful life in the country:
to get away from it all, they said.

You could say they were escaping
to a preferred reality,
    their idea of the ideal. For them
the good life was to be found outside the city,

near a river, or by the sea, with trees
and hills on the skyline
    above which the moon swelled
and made them feel the world was benign.

Ducks quacked in a pond in a paddock nearby.
Starlight flashed there, and a few frogs
    croaked happily in the moonlight. Ah.
After a few years the city caught up

with them so they sold out to sub-dividers
and made a killing. Now there's
    farther to go to snare one's
piece of paradise: houses stud the hills

they used to signal to when talking
of the glories of unspoiled nature.
    They live, today, in a townhouse
within easy walking distance of a park

in which there is a duck pond
and feathered friends that gladly receive
    the contents of their plastic bags
of stale bread; and none look to the hills.

Documentaries about Tomorrow's World

Breath, the battles between nature and nurture,
taxes, then death, then the faxes to faraway places
saying you weren't worth a fortune, that most
of what you owned was worth sweet fuck all
although the bits and pieces clearly meant
something of importance at one time or another.

Is that not the way, is that not how it is?

The safest place to be is somewhere
in between so-called winning and losing,
watching the arrival of another spring,
the trees in bud, the perkiness of the first pollies,
the sunny daffies, a time when all you
prefer to think about is faith and hope.

It's better than warbling on about there being
no guarantees while listening to a blackbird
arguing over scraps with wax-eyes
while on the radio Kim Hill is questioning
an exceedingly clever bugger about physics,
quantum mechanics, the elegance of string theory
and all that, someone famous, a national treasure
who knows even more than she does, but only just.

They agree that tomorrow's world
will be a much different, but not necessarily
better, place. Who would argue with that?
Ask the nor'wester in the pine trees,
ask the snow-melt in the Ida Burn,
ask the last of the sunlight
golden on the pleats of the Hawkdun range.
Ask anyone but a bleeding heart
who thinks his days are numbered.

Shareholders' Meeting

No one's actually filing in with a broad smile
    and a spring in their step, suggesting
most of the buggers know far more than me.

A few are apt to say, 'Hope springs eternal',
    just for a laugh, like, and when
the chairman asserts, 'This company has great

potential going forward', as if he believed
    some of the shareholders might be
concerned the firm had the potential 'to fall

over in the face of vigorous competition
    from the tigers offshore', there are
a few whimperings and sniggers around where

I am sitting anyway. 'The economy's
    slowing,' the chairman says, 'the heat's
gone out of it.' Papers shuffle and a guy

next to me fidgets, says 'I smell a rat',
    another way of saying *someone's*
farted in church. As we are leaving

after hearing that 'the prospects look good
    in the longterm and there's nothing to be
too concerned about', a stranger asks me,

'Do you think we should get out now?'
    Ah, all I can think of is, though
I'm not the right person to ask, who is?

Gilt Edge

The well-groomed man told us we needed
to take steps to secure our future,

that there was a new float coming up
well worth looking at, and that we were

advised to get in quickly as, going forward,
the prospects were highly promising.

We could expect a good yield. It occurred
that you'd grown used to yielding:

with Telecom and Feltex you yielded
big time, but that's in line with the lose some

win some, always spread your risks advice
experts offer, and yet you still felt like

a right pillock, shafted again. Of course
there are no guarantees, the expert said,

and wittered on about ways to guard yourself . . .
At one point he even mentioned leverage,

who had it and who didn't, or something
like that – you were drifting then – but you had

to admire the nerve of one who contrived to look
both confident and wistful at the same time.

Pawns in the Game

He told me quietly, earnestly,
ubiquitous and equivocal to the end,
a conspirator from way back,

that, in respect to most things,
it was hard to decide which was right
and which wrong. *I could hear*

a mouse scratching in the wall,
and the wailing of the wind
in the pines, and water laughing

in the taps. We talked of a time
and a place for all things,
what's appropriate, or not,

as is said, *in the circumstances;*
and of social splinters
like calls for cultural safety,

sensitivity, not giving offence . . .
on and on like men with tambourines
who think their enthusiasm's

shared by all and sundry, as if they're
as special as sun-dried tomatoes
in a town without a deli.

'Of course you have to remember
we're instruments,' he said,
'pawns in the game. We're like warp

and weft; we give shit and eat shit.
All the world's a rage, and being
tendentious is what we do best.'

He might as well have said
life's all about communication, tolerance,
inclusion, going forward not back.

I could smell a rat in the ceiling,
hear cockroaches in the hot water cupboard,
wind huffing and puffing under the eaves,

and water still laughing in the taps.

Basic Instincts

I'm assuming the hawk tearing flesh
    from a rabbit's carcass
in the middle of the road
    in a searing cold westerly

doesn't complain about
    a lack of cell phone reception,
the absence of restaurants
    in the area, or screech

about rights, extol the virtues
    of the free market
and express a belief in the presence
    of an invisible hand.

I presume the bird would rather
    not be run over by me
and that only one of us is worried
    about how one deals

with such realities as the burden of guilt,
    ethical behaviour, sexual infidelity,
religious conviction, racial prejudice,
    public opinion polls and man's,

what was that again, 'inhumanity to man'.

A PM in the High Country

The PM walks in the high country
where only the wind blows hard,
nothing's snide, tub-thumping
gets you nowhere, and nothing's
contorted by certitude or censure.

She is alone and possibly lonely
in the way that milling clouds aren't.

Here, there's no political mileage
in point-scoring, in tantrums:
a breath of fresh air means
exactly that, and the only whip
you need to avoid is matagouri
in a place where approval ratings
don't count. It's where, if you vowed
to go down fighting, all you'd hear
was scree clapping and the hissing
of the wind in the tussock. Is it
too late for her to be de-bugged?

Up High

If you took away music
and the pure deep blue of the
Central sky, what then? If you
eroded the sureties of
politicians who argue
they have solutions that none
have thought of before, who would
object? If you took away
the blue-grey afternoon light
on the snow-striped Hawkduns,
and the Sibelian sounds geese
make up high, think of that, *that*.

High Society

Oh, all that skin, all that sheen, all that glitter,
jewellery boxes on the move; and oh, the teeth, serried rows
of blinging white. Why can't they keep their mouths shut?

Hunkered Down

When Stephen Dobyns writes of a man
who decides he 'will run away and immigrate
to New Zealand' with 'his friend's daughter',
and tells us his intention
is 'to raise sheep and children',
it's almost as if he's *baaing* about
the desire to *experience another culture,*
see the world through others' eyes,
get inside another's skin.

The couple will have been living,
says Dobyns, in 'a little log house',
a reminder, possibly, of sketches of cabins
in forests on the edge of the prairie
when life was harder and simpler
than today. But one man's hankering
is another's horror. I'm hunkered down
here, determined to stay,
fighting to escape being fleeced.

Homecoming

My friend said there was always a big gap
between him and his son, *right from the start,*
and there still is. I asked him where the boy was now.

I think he's in America, he said, *working for*
a currency trading outfit or something like that.
Two days later the boy came home, a surprise

visit, with a barbie look-alike in tow: his
future wife. Later, my friend told me he *should*
have known this would happen, a bimbo.

You'd have thought the woman was Eurydice
except the son was no Orpheus; he borrowed a bike
and a helmet and lycra-clad set off round the bays

the very next day, *for old time's sake,* he said.

v

Gryphon

The things you
dare not
and the things
you ought
to do, staccato
through
and through.

And the wretched
insufferable
souls who harp
and hector,
say you should
do this, you
should do that.

They are like
gryphons
eroding on sills
who were hunched
there centuries
before you were
born and will

still be there
when you are
gone. You should
have been a
gryphon, a creature
there never was,
set in stone.

High Windows

If you want to compliment someone call him grounded.
If you want to do him a favour
pray that there's more order than chaos, more love

than hatred and resentment in his life, that
transfiguration and redemption are acquaintances,
at least, and possibly friends. Let him be

wistful rather than woeful when looking out of high windows.
Allow him to prance, say he knew wonder and joy
and turned his back on the place called Last Resort.

Let him believe he told the truth, most of the time.

Umbrella

When you hear of older sods
reflecting on, and accounting for,
their idiot youth, musing

it was because they saw themselves
as bullet proof, you're bemused.
To you, youth was fear, fragility,

the future a fog rolling in at twilight
time. Nothing seemed benign
or rosy for long: dark clouds

massed. An umbrella furled by the door.

Just About Complete

I have a friend who's drawn to the idea *complete,*
who prefers that to the blunt monosyllable *end,*
suggesting there's fear inherent in a phrase like
the end in mind, and disbelief in the clanging
end of the matter. In the end it matters little,
one supposes, for end is end, and then
there's no point in discussing the distance
between ambivalence and indeterminate . . .

so one goes for *complete,* for its sense
of dignity, order, maybe even grace,
like the aura surrounding those who walk
as if their feet barely touch and never pound
the ground, and whose faces never appear
supercilious as the moon's shine on water
when you think what you're seeing
will never be quite so beguiling again.

Considerations

1

When I had more of a future
I couldn't see it for the present
rushing by. It's not what one knows,
it's what's meant when you wonder
if we'd be better off
with fewer promises to keep.

Expectations mangle; is that
the mark of the human condition?

2

All those columns about 24 hours
of wowee where everything's
marvellous – gutsing and drinking lots
at an airline's expense, say,
or a travel agent's – but nothing's new
except the claims that we're
being given the dinkum oil
on the *real* Fiji, or Venice, or Rome.
Let the pampered bastards
broil in Bali, melt on the Gold Coast,
then come home and shut up
about what passes as worthwhile,
pleasurable to them.

3

I live among caboodles who believe
we can improve on nature
and have a duty to do so
if we are to prosper. So much power
and no harm done? Come now,
when material anxieties
become manifest greed

how does the essence of place
escape corruption, survive?

4
A Central Otago prayer:
Let the sun shine
on the Old Man Range,
the snow's melt-water
flow pure and clear,
and the winds of summer
blow benign; and let
things good and kind
prevail
more often
than not
in a landscape
that's still to experience
more proper love
and respect.

5
More and Better
are not always
birds of a feather.

6
For New Year Resolution
read
built-in obsolescence.

7
Ask yourself to whom
rectitude and pride
mean more, the rich
or the poor?

8
My mother, well past 80,
says, 'I can't sit down
for too long because it aches,
and I can't stand
for too long because
it's too tiring. What do you do?'

She answers that:
'You carry on.'

9
Round here the clarity of the light
startles like nowhere else
I've been. You'd think
we'd have seen more than we have.

10
Fashion, craft, make it wrought
but don't delude yourself
that it is final.

11
Darwin thought that for many
'ignorance more frequently
begets confidence
than does knowledge',
but he didn't say it was an excuse
unless, one supposes, you
don't know what's gone missing.

12
It doesn't follow
that because someone's
got more money
than you
they are smarter,
but they may have

more options
and fewer true friends.

13
The poor crave respect,
the wealthy buy deference.
Where admiration
or concern comes from
is harder to ascertain.

14
What lasts isn't what is last
of the last, it's what
you won't be seeing
unless you have the sense
to sense it.

15
My son, in London, who works
trying to rehabilitate
sick people, is on 25,000 pounds
or thereabouts, a year.

Bankers on 'basics'
of four times that,
and bonuses
'in good years' of
hundreds of thousands more,
work with money.
Go figure.

16
Be serious
and someone
will say
you're silly,
or that they don't
want moral missives

from someone
presuming
to be wise.

As if anyone
thinks they know
it all. Besides,
some people like silly.
Who are you
to say it's not
wise, or silly?
Silly.

17
I've heard it said
poetry and poets
are hard to understand,
to live with. Who isn't?

They think too much,
I've been told, about
things better left
alone. Which things
are those?

18
Arousal erases
what you'd sooner
have retained.

Nice for all that.

19
Nature, as we perceive it,
is what grows in us
and whose influence
makes for compulsion.

It's the striving to be *at one*
with what you can't,
and yet, you and it may be
the better for it. A

good enough reason,
then, to make the effort.
It's the way the inside's
affected by the outside,

and what gets in
and stays there
like seed in the earth
for decades and more.

20
Grief and guilt are twins.
The more you know about
the one the more you learn
about parts of the self
you wish weren't yours.

It's a case of deciding
which preoccupations
are helpful, and who
to turn to for help.
Then again, who said

definitions are definitive?
if that's what you'd like
to know. Be warned,
derision's face is as
featureless as a balloon

hovering above your head,
the light reflecting
like a sneer. Think
about what that means.
That will do for now.

Relationship Services

When the wind returned and clouds
slid across from the west
and smothered the stars
and the autumn leaves began to panic
you remembered the time when
you heard a therapist say solemnly
that we needed to accept
that sex and love were not synonymous
as if any adult was unaware of that

Celebrity

On a blue day
    when you're anything but blue
and the sun's as sharp as a sprag
  it's easy to forget fate

and what befalls those
    who shake the hand of a stranger
whose back's to the sun;
  the stranger who is

the consciousness of our time
    whenever conscience comes calling
and won't go away.
  Everyone knows her name.

Levity

When levity dances with grace in mind,
desperation looking over her shoulder,
pathos is always in the audience,
leaning on a pillar, standing tall
in shadow at the back of the hall.

And flippancy's the mask both wear
to cover brute contempt. Mostly
there's no need for a go-between
when the medium is cabaret
and the message is about decay,

who's in, who's on the way out.

Liberty

I went to school today, by the river,
in the sunshine, snowmelt
greening the water in the pools,

the music of the ripples
straight out of the works of Granados.
So what did I learn at school today?

That there's nothing quite like
the music of water from the mountains
if you care about liberty.

Aren't We All

1
Joe, I said, with a smile
on my face and a
mandolin plunking
in my heart, is a
surprise on the way?

Sonny, he said, patting
my head, just write
and see what happens,
see what drives you
and where you are

driven. And I thought,
not for the first time,
of finales, that these
are worrying times.

2
You and me,
there's acoustic.

If you stop
hearing it,

or I do, the
music's over.

3
Turn away from those
who ask you what you'd do
if you had your life
over again, as if it's true
that much doesn't go
according to plan, as if you

hadn't faced up to
the reality. Which is
things could have been
better or worse;
you could have pulled
a few more rabbits
out of hats and stopped
howling at the moon
like an old huntaway
left behind, who probably
senses *all over* is not
far away.

4
Beauty's not truth,
it's not terrible,
it's what's unbidden
that strikes
but doesn't stain.

It's what you think
you'll never forget
each time you say
that's the most beautiful
thing you've ever seen.

Hereafter

There's this noise that sounds as if
    longing's somewhere inside
as well as farther off, in an old shed,
    perhaps, where nests are wedged
between rafters and the roof like tumours.

The shed's been evacuated, is slowly
    collapsing, and you cannot,
would not dare say there was bound
    to be a time when love was in the air
like motes here, because someone

might ask you to define it. But it's
    something like *all in* without
conditions, isn't it? Something that
    brings tears to your eyes, something
that seems like a matter of supreme importance,

something that sleeps alongside grief
    and humiliation, and conspires
to be up and away before they wake,
    something that isn't vestigial memory,
something that doesn't make you wonder

whether what devoured you years ago,
    when you were another man
but the same man in another skin,
    was actually love or simply that messy
casserole of lust and infatuation.

Yes, or no, or whatever, what matters
    matters, mattered then, matters now.
Matters more than any of the words
    that you can find with which to say it.
That's what love is: it's what matters

most at the time, this time. Love, it's
        a kingdom of difference whose boundaries
shift and shake: it's where we come from
        before we leave and set out in spirit
for what is said to be even more heavenly

as long as belief is heartfelt and one's faith
        is unswerving but not imperious.
Whenever and whatever, conviction's
        likely more help than hindrance,
possibly allows us to say maybe our end's

just to drift away like milt in the eddying
        mystical mystery that is whatever
comes next, that nowhere in particular
        some think of as the hereafter,
longed-for, and longed-for and longed-for . . .

Flutter

Memory's memory flutters in the attic,
scrabbles, looks for a way out
into the radiant open air, wants to fly off
wings edged in gold, feathers ruffled
by the breath of the Gods.

In the meantime this summertime
your memory of others is hazy,
random, like seeds scattered
from a pod snapped by the heat
and force of sun and wind.

It's hard to carry loads of grief
in the summertime, the freight of
dead stars consigned to sidings
in vacant corners of the sky
where the wagons are hidden away

like the souls of those who can't
or don't want to remember what happened
to the sheets of happiness
stained by hurt and whatever else
is in the lap of the Gods.

Enduring Love

I'd take enduring love
before most other swats
any time, but only if
it brought divinity's promises,
those we could have faith in.

I'd still pray though
for bloodlines reliable
and visions of paradise
in all its ample glory.
And there, where play

is work when not illusion,
whimsy gives way
to reverence and love,
and nothing else matters
quite as much, or more.

Morning After a Storm

I can't stop watching
the slow migration east
of milky-white cumulus
on a dying westerly.
They form, disperse,
reform, then drift apart
as we do when hearts
and minds quarrel.
So it goes.
          The breeze
wiffles my new-washed
hair that's whitening
fast. Orange blossom's
emerged from the shelter
of a stumpy conifer
and everywhere I turn
birds are impudent,
wary, urgent, snickery,
chittery, excited
by song. I could ask
for more, but not today.

Matukituki

When rock breaks through the skin of the land
it's truth baring itself, and you're reminded
how honesty's a face which tears stream down
like rain that stains as often as it cleanses.

These mountain walls say *We shall not be moved
by mere mortals*, and when shadows
creep over them they move as if to prove
there are wraiths in stone that none can restrain.

Day and night they listen to the river's refrain.

Backwards

Walk backwards and the past
unfolds in front of you. That way

you learn the truth, or discover it,
for the first time, perhaps.

Even then, though, interpretation
or a preference for a particular

version might rule the day. And
if that seems likely, then

you probably knew the truth
all along, and you would have

no need to walk backwards
ever again, eagerly or with

apprehension in your heart,
away from the land of the living.

Such is Life

We talk, somehow, and someone translates.
Let it be true. As when we used to be happy,
in a fashion, to have a house to live in.
Just about any old place, brick or weatherboard
would do, a place to call home, if not one's own.

There was washing flapping in a southerly,
a grandmother for whom *blessed*
was as close to swearing as she ever dared go,
stock passing in crates
destined for the Burnside works, a corner store
that delivered groceries to the back door,
Mum pleased with the size of her spuds
and tickled pink to have a bumper crop of currants
for once.
    Waste not, want not. And in the evenings
the whole family singing of taking high roads
or low roads to the very same place in the end,
Mum with tears in her eyes
for reasons I never
fully understood and never will.

Tool Kit

Restraint, resolve, reliability . . .
you might not fall in love
with that trio, but you could

live with them. Add in some
benign mischief-making
and not too much that's

laced with wistfulness and
that shouldn't be too hard
to swallow. Like tact that's

not devious, it could even work
as a pick-me-up, leave you
with a fair idea of what to take

seriously and what to eschew.
Might as well pay attention, learn
a few new tricks along the way.

The Earth is Enough
(after Geoffrey Gurrumul Yunupingu)

You listen to a blind man singing
what only the lucky can see
and you've a feeling you're
missing something he is not

let what's constant be reassuring
not dull   and let time slow

for you like it the way
there's a rhythm
in the waves of the land
and in the clouds

looking for a way
out of the sky   and the light

so bright all day
is fading   soft
oh dulcet air and airs
you touch us inside

and out and you don't ever
want them to leave you alone

there must be some
who believe the earth is enough
who think of anthems
of refuge   of wonder   of peace